TABLE OF CONTENTS

MOVING PLATES

MINERALS

ROCKS

GEMS

GEODES

THE THIRD ROCK FROM THE SUN

Whether we see them or not, rocks are constantly under our feet or sometimes rising far above us as mountains. They are products of a much bigger rock, this "third rock from the Sun" we call Earth. That's why understanding rocks, **minerals**, **geodes**, and gems helps us understand our planet.

We live on Earth's crust, its thinnest layer, which is made largely of **igneous** rock. (More about igneous rock on page 16.) Just beneath that is the thicker upper mantle, which is solid rock close to the surface and **molten** rock farther down.

Then comes the lower mantle—which stays solid, despite the heat, because of pressure. At the very center of our planet are the metallic outer core and solid inner core, with temperatures hundreds to thousands of times hotter than on the surface.

ROCK-HARD FACT

Earth is a giant ball of rock weighing about 6 sextillion (that's 6 followed by 21 zeros) tons (5.4 sextillion tonnes). Our planet's rock layers go hundreds of miles deep.

MOVING PLATES

Scientists believe Earth's surface is made up of floating plates of rock. These plates always move a little—so little we can't feel it. But when they move a lot, they collide and cause volcanic eruptions or earthquakes. Our planet has about 1,500 active **volcanoes**, many under the sea, with 50 to 80 eruptions a year. Every day, hundreds of minor earthquakes take place, with at least one major quake somewhere in the world each month.

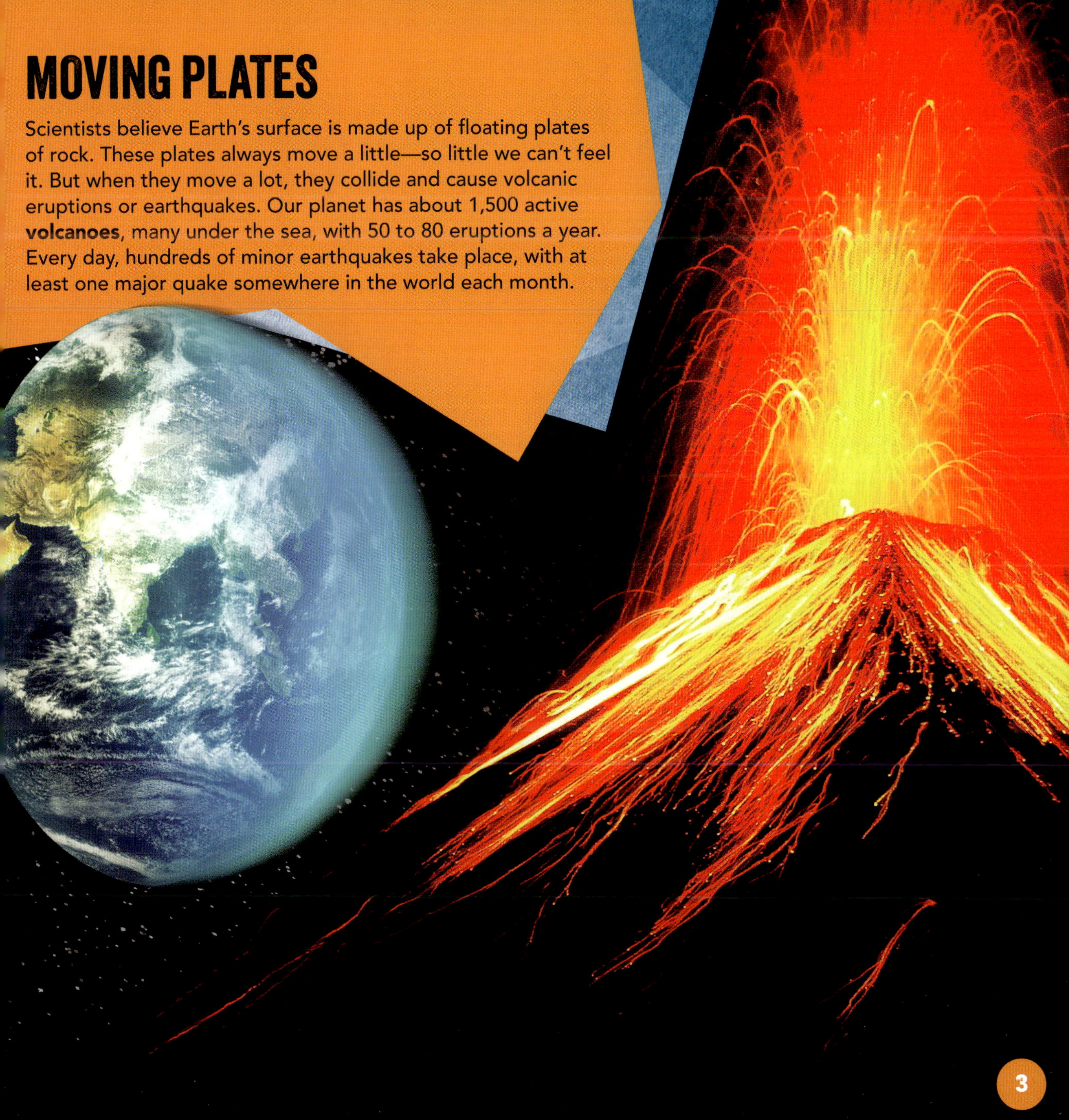

IT ALL STARTS WITH MINERALS

The atomic number for gold is 79.

79
Au
Gold 196.96

Minerals are the building blocks of rocks and gems. They're made of **atoms** arranged in a **uniform** pattern. Just like humans, who have one-of-a-kind DNA and fingerprints, minerals have certain properties that make them unique. Their properties result from their **composition** and how their atoms are arranged.

MAGNETITE

GRAPHITE

GOLD

1

TALC

2

GYPSUM

3

CALCITE

SOFT

4

FLUORITE

5

APATITE

MEDIUM

SIX PROPERTIES OF MINERALS

Minerals have special features called properties that make them different from one another. Let's look at six of them.

1 Specific gravity: How heavy is it compared with the same amount of water?

2 Luster: Is it shiny or dull?

SHINY

PYRITE

CINNABAR

DULL

3 Transparency: Can you shine a flashlight through it?

AMBER

4 Hardness: Is it soft enough to scratch with a fingernail or another rock, or does it leave a scratch mark behind instead?

5 Color: What color is it?

FUCHSITE

HEMATITE

6 Streak: When you rub it across a rough surface, what color streak does it make? The streak test shows the mineral's true color. For instance, the mineral hematite can appear black, white, red, or silver. But you can identify it by its red streak.

AQUAMARINE

MOHS SCALE OF HARDNESS

Minerals are assigned numbers according to their hardness.

6

ORTHOCLASE

7

QUARTZ

8

TOPAZ

9

CORUNDUM

10

DIAMOND

HARD

DARE TO COMPARE

Geologists and **mineralogists** learn about rocks and minerals by studying them. Let's put your rocks to the test and see what you can learn about them.

1 **Magnetism:** Is your rock drawn to a magnet? If so, it contains the mineral iron.

2 **Floating:** Drop your rock into a plastic cup filled with water. If your rock floats, you have a **porous** igneous rock.

3 **Hardness:** Try to scratch your rock with your fingernail. Then scratch it against another rock. Whichever one is most easily scratched is the softest according to the Mohs scale. The one that leaves the most scratch marks is the hardest.

4 **Streak test:** With an adult's help, find a single white tile, or use the bottom of a white ceramic coffee mug. Rub your rock on the dull, or unglazed, side of it. Does the streak color match the rock color, or is it different? The streak shows you the rock's true color.

5 **Luster:** Wash your rock with warm water, and let it air dry. Is it shiny? If so, it has luster. A rock with luster sometimes contains a type of metal.

6 **Transparency:** Hold a flashlight behind your rock. If the light shines through it, your rock is transparent. If it doesn't, your rock is **opaque**.

ROCK-HARD FACT

Made from pure carbon, diamonds were once considered the hardest material in the world. We now know that diamonds are softer than wurtzite boron nitride and lonsdaleite, but those materials are so rare that diamonds still take center stage.

HOW DO YOUR ROCKS RANK?

	IS IT MAGNETIC?		DOES IT FLOAT?		HOW HARD IS IT?	WHAT'S ITS TRUE COLOR?	DOES IT HAVE LUSTER?		IS IT TRANSPARENT?	
	CIRCLE ONE		CIRCLE ONE		SOFTEST: 1 HARDEST: 4		CIRCLE ONE		CIRCLE ONE	
1	Y	N	Y	N			Y	N	Y	N
2	Y	N	Y	N			Y	N	Y	N
3	Y	N	Y	N			Y	N	Y	N
4	Y	N	Y	N			Y	N	Y	N

STRANGE-BUT-TRUE STORIES

MIND-BLOWING MERCURY

The Mad Hatter of *Alice in Wonderland* was inspired by fact, and you can blame mercury for his strange behavior. Mercury, a mineral and **element** usually found in liquid form, is used in thermometers and science. It was also used as medicine—until it was found to be **toxic**.

In the 1800s, mercury was used to improve the felt used in hat making. Before mercury, hatmakers used urine! The problem was that mercury made hatmakers drool, talk to themselves, and shake, prompting the term "mad as a hatter."

COLOR-CHANGING MINERALS

Some minerals may change color under ultraviolet light. Autunite changes from a yellowish color to a spooky green. Even spookier, it glows because it's **radioactive**! It contains the element uranium, used in making bombs and generating power.

This glowing effect is called **fluorescence**, a term named after the mineral fluorite. Fluorite may be the most colorful mineral of them all. It can even change color under sunlight or appear to have bands of color.

Other minerals—like amazonite and labradorite—seem to change colors when viewed from different angles. This changing ability is known as **iridescence**.

LABRADORITE

AMAZONITE

ROCK-HARD FACT

Strange as it sounds, recycling electronic devices can protect gorillas, chimpanzees, and elephants. When the metallic mineral coltan—used in electronics—is mined in parts of Africa, their habitat may be destroyed. If coltan is recycled, less needs to be mined, resulting in less destruction of habitats.

Do you ever wonder how animals have such a good sense of direction, giving them the ability to travel hundreds or even thousands of miles to specific locations? They can thank the mineral magnetite, which is found in their brains. It gives them an ability known as **magnetoreception**, which helps them create mental maps to their destinations.

COMMON MINERALS

Minerals are always solid. When a mineral turns liquid from heat, it stops being a mineral. Minerals form when **magma** melts and cools beneath Earth's surface. Water evaporates, leaving behind minerals in crystal form. Let's get to know some of the most common minerals.

QUARTZ

FELDSPAR

QUARTZ

Quartz is another key ingredient in Earth's crust, and it may be the most useful mineral of all. It's used widely in watches and electronics because it can release an electrical charge and act as a battery. Some gemstones, such as amethyst and citrine, are made of quartz.

CITRINE

AMETHYST

FELDSPAR

More feldspar is found in Earth's crust than any other mineral. Most of the rocks found in the crust—rocks like granite and basalt—contain feldspar. It is found in every category of rock, including in gemstones.

MICA

Found in lesser amounts in the crust, mica forms in flat sheets. It scores a mere 2.5 on the Mohs scale, so you can scratch it with your fingernail. If you ever visit Mount Rushmore National Memorial in South Dakota, you'll get a firsthand look at rocks containing mica.

MICA

MINERAL FEAST

Minerals are found in many things other than rocks. They're also found in food. Beef, for instance, contains the mineral iron. Bananas are a good source of potassium, and dairy is a good source of calcium. These minerals, along with others, help our bodies grow and stay healthy.

BRIDGMANITE

Scientists think a mineral with a similar composition to olivine, known as bridgmanite, makes up more than one-third of Earth's entire volume. They believe this from studying meteorites, which form under amounts of pressure and heat similar to what is found in our planet's mantle.

OLIVINE

ROCK-HARD FACT

About a third of the water we drink comes from within underground rock. Minerals from rocks strengthen our bodies and help water taste better.

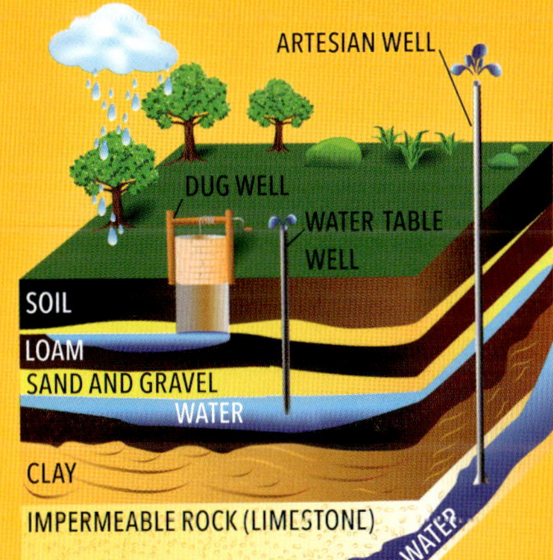

STRANGE-BUT-TRUE STORIES
CAN MINERALS ZAP POLLUTION?

In the 1940s, geologists unearthed minerals from a Siberian mine. For a long time, scientists lacked the tools to test them properly. But finally in 2010, a **chemistry** professor read an article from an old magazine about the minerals.

The professor noticed the Siberian minerals sounded a lot like man-made materials that had only been made in laboratories. No one had believed anything like these materials could be found in nature.

Scientists believe the minerals, now named stepanovite and zhemchuzhnikovite, can work like sponges that can soak up carbon gases in our air. A discovery like that could greatly improve our air quality and protect our environment. Scientists also think the minerals could be used to create energy. They hope to find other natural sources of the minerals and test their **theories**.

ZHEMCHUZHNIKOVITE

CHANGING EARTH'S LAYERS

Geologists learn a lot about Earth's history by studying its **strata**. The layers tell stories of earthquakes and volcanoes, ancient animals and plants, the people who once lived here, and even the **climate**. Scientists try to figure out when events happened or when things or people lived.

Some scientists fear the strata from modern times will send a confusing message to future geologists. Building materials today can come from all over the world. Once they break down, they will create a mash of minerals not typically found in that part of the world.

Imagine, for instance, the Washington Monument as a column of limestone within the earth where no other limestone can be found. Add to that a number of man-made minerals scattered about. Future layers could become even more confusing.

ROCK-HARD FACT

Most mineral crystals are so tiny you can only see them with a microscope. But some are larger than people. The Cave of the Crystals in Chihuahua, Mexico, is home to record-breaking selenite columns measuring 36 feet (11 m) long, 4 feet (1.2 m) wide, and weighing about 55 tons (50 t) each.

Scientists were stumped by rocks and boulders made of the mineral dolomite that seemed to propel themselves across Racetrack Playa in Death Valley National Park. In 2014, they used cameras to solve the mystery. The playa—covered in 3 inches (8 cm) of water—would freeze overnight. As the sun rose, the cracking ice and wind sent the rocks sailing.

ROCK YOUR WORLD

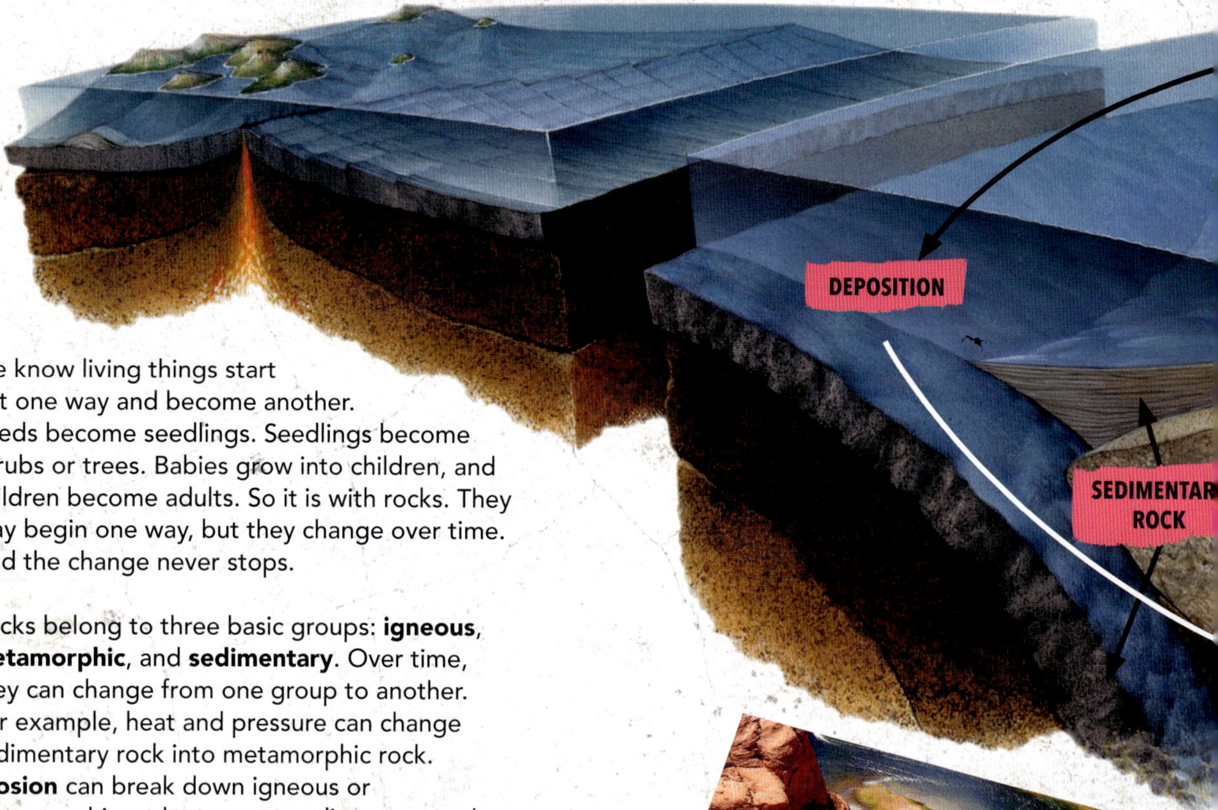

DEPOSITION

SEDIMENTAR
ROCK

We know living things start out one way and become another. Seeds become seedlings. Seedlings become shrubs or trees. Babies grow into children, and children become adults. So it is with rocks. They may begin one way, but they change over time. And the change never stops.

Rocks belong to three basic groups: **igneous**, **metamorphic**, and **sedimentary**. Over time, they can change from one group to another. For example, heat and pressure can change sedimentary rock into metamorphic rock. **Erosion** can break down igneous or metamorphic rock to create sedimentary rock. And deep underground, metamorphic rock can melt into magma, which might eventually cool to become igneous rock.

These and other changes create the rock cycle. Some parts of the cycle, such as the forming of igneous rock during a volcanic eruption, happen quickly. Other parts, such as the buildup of sedimentary rock, can take millions of years.

HORSESHOE BEND, COLORADO RIVER

THE ROCK CYCLE

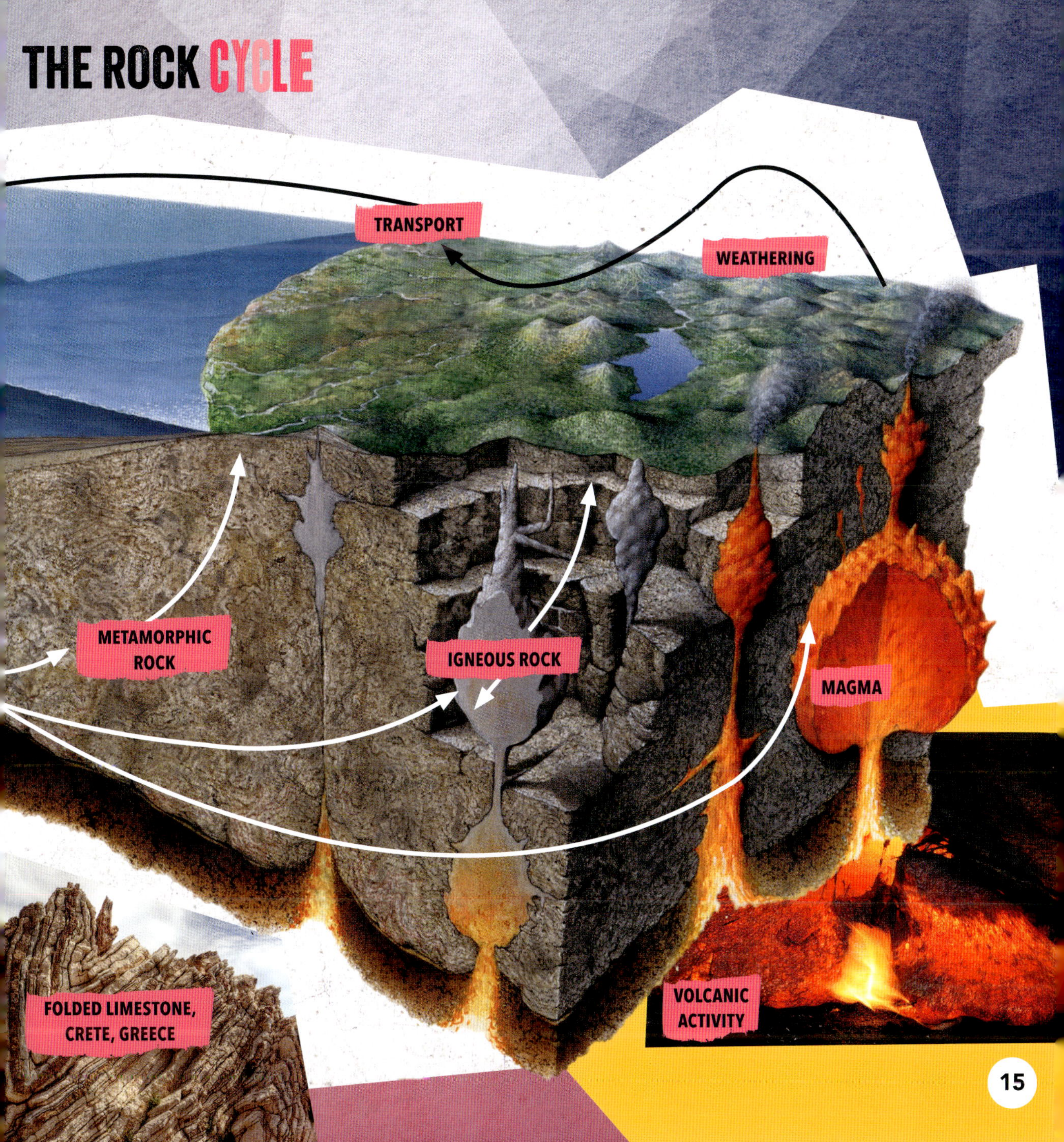

IGNEOUS ROCKS

Igneous rocks form belowground or on Earth's surface when molten rock cools to become solid. Underground, molten material cools slowly to create **intrusive** rocks. When magma escapes through surface cracks or volcanoes, it becomes lava and cools into **extrusive** rocks.

Though sedimentary rocks are found more often on the surface, igneous rocks are actually the most common type of rock. Igneous rocks—with more than 700 different types—make up most of Earth's upper crust.

IGNEOUS ROCK TYPES

EXTRUSIVE IGNEOUS ROCK
Magma comes out as lava and cools on the surface

INTRUSIVE IGNEOUS ROCK
Magma cools beneath Earth's surface

INTRUSIVE ROCKS

OBSIDIAN
RHYOLITE
EXTRUSIVE ROCKS
PUMICE
SCORIA
ANDESITE

SEDIMENTARY ROCKS

Sedimentary rocks are easy to spot: Just look for layers. Like pages in a book, layers tell a story about the rock's formation.

First, erosion breaks down rocks into sediment, like sand or mud. Over time, layers of sediment build up. The weight of the layers on top presses on the layers below, turning them to rock.

Sometimes the remains of living things—plants or animals—are buried within the layers. Sedimentary rocks that contain living things are **organic**, and rocks that don't contain living things are **inorganic**.

When plant or animal parts are trapped in sediment before they rot, they can slowly turn to rock, becoming **fossils**. Footprints and leaf prints can harden to become imprint fossils. We learn about life and the climate in the past by studying fossils.

GRAINS OF BEACH SAND

COMPRESSED LAYERS OF SEDIMENT

FOSSILIZED SHARK TOOTH

FOSSILIZED FOOTPRINTS

ORGANIC
SEDIMENTARY
ROCKS
COAL
COQUINA
LIMESTONE
LIMESTONE
OIL SHALE
INORGANIC
SEDIMENTARY
ROCKS
CHERT
GYPSUM
FLINT
SILTSTONE

METAMORPHIC ROCKS

When something morphs, it changes—like the way a fictional robot morphs into a vehicle. Metamorphic rocks don't become robots or vehicles, but they change in really amazing ways as a result of heat, pressure, and **chemical** changes.

These changes often take place deep underground or where Earth's plates crash together. The makeup of the rock changes slowly without it melting. Later, erosion and uplift caused by Earth's moving plates can push metamorphic rocks to the surface, often around mountains. You can spot them by the twists, swirls, and folds within them.

Because the rock cycle never ends, metamorphic rocks can begin as igneous rocks, break down into sedimentary rocks, and eventually become metamorphic rocks.

SCHIST
GNEISS
QUARTZITE
RED MARBLE

CONGLOMERATE ROCKS

Conglomerate rocks are like the blended families of the rock world. They are a special type of sedimentary rock that can contain rounded pieces of sedimentary, igneous, or metamorphic rock held together by sand or mud.

Rocks are carried for a long distance by a river or ocean currents. The rocks get broken down and their edges smoothed over time. Then sand or mud fills in the gaps between the rocks, eventually hardening to form conglomerate rock.

Because they're held together by sand or mud, these rocks can be easily broken. That means they can easily reform all over again. Geologists sometimes study conglomerate rocks in an area; if the rocks contain valuable minerals, such as gold or diamonds, that can indicate whether more of those minerals are nearby.

CONGLOMERATE ROCK

MEET AN IMPOSTER

At first glance, breccia looks like a conglomerate rock. It does, after all, contain pieces of rock held together by a type of natural cement. But there's a small difference: The pieces within breccia are angular, while the pieces within conglomerates are round. Breccia forms from rubble that hasn't been smoothed by the action of water.

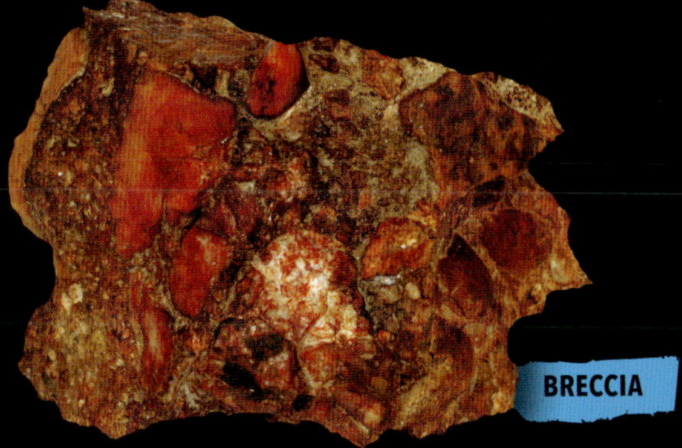

BRECCIA

MARS

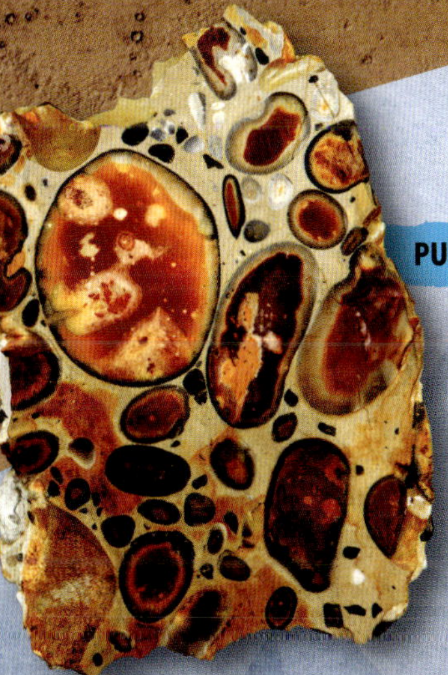

PUDDING STONE

Pudding stones are conglomerate rocks with dark pebbles held together by lighter sand or mud.

A CLUE TO THE HISTORY OF MARS

A NASA rover found evidence that water was once on the surface of Mars. The evidence: a bed of conglomerate rocks that could have been moved only by water. Scientists believe where there is water, there may be life.

STRANGE-BUT-TRUE STORIES
THE WORLD'S WEIRDEST ROCK FORMATIONS

Sometimes underground limestone dissolves away, creating sinkholes aboveground. Sinkholes can form suddenly, and houses, cars, and even people can get sucked inside.

Sinkholes in the ocean can be beautiful, as proven by the Great Blue Hole off the coast of Belize. This massive sinkhole measures 984 feet (300 m) across and 407 feet (124 m) deep. Divers explore it to see the **marine** life within it.

Over many years, flash flood waters full of sandy debris have carved spectacular shapes into the soft sandstone of Antelope Canyon.

GREAT BLUE HOLE, BELIZE

ANTELOPE CANYON, ARIZONA

THE ORIGINAL STATE OF THE SUNSHINE STATE

Most of us can easily find Florida on a map. It's that long fingerlike state—the one with all the sunshine, water, and great vacation spots. But long ago, finding Florida might not have been as easy as heading south from Georgia.

In fact, Florida might not have been in what became the United States, or even in North America. Scientists say the rocks beneath Florida show it was originally part of Africa or South America. They believe two plates beneath the surface crashed together, causing Florida to break off and attach itself to North America. Will the Sunshine State stay put? Only time will tell.

ROCK-HARD FACT

For thousands of years, these huge columns of stone—most upright, with others laid across the tops of them—have mystified scientists. Some of the stones weigh 4.4 tons (4 t). How did they get there? What was their purpose? The site, known as Stonehenge, is a popular tourist destination in Great Britain and still remains a mystery.

In the 1970s, a man named Gary Dahl made $15 million selling a new type of pet that came in a cardboard box with a bed of straw inside. This pet didn't eat, poop, play, or require attention of any kind. So what was this miracle pet? It was a pet rock. Dahl priced his pet rocks at $3.95 each, selling one million in 1975 alone.

START YOUR OWN ROCK COLLECTION

Starting your own rock collection is fun and easy. Here are a few tips for getting started:

Identify sources. With an adult's help, research what types of rocks can be found in your area. Do you live near mountains, a river or stream, a lake, or an ocean? All those areas will offer a wealth of rock samples.

Get a few basic tools. You'll need a backpack, work gloves, goggles, a rock hammer, a rock chisel, a magnifying glass, a camera or cell phone, and sturdy shoes. Also remember to pack plenty of water and snacks!

Be observant and take notes. Take pictures of each sample as you find it. Assign it a number, and write down what you observe about it and where you found it.

Clean rocks carefully. Wash them in warm water and mild soap. Use a soft brush to scrub off excess dirt. Let them air-dry.

Store and label your samples. Store each rock separately in an egg carton, and identify it by its type (if you know what it is) or by its number using sticky labels.

Study your rocks. Note how they compare in hardness. What can you observe about their properties? (See pages 6–7.)

Find a local geology or mineralogy club. There's strength in numbers! Ask an adult to help you find a club so you can learn more about collecting and identifying rocks.

Ask a professional for help. If identifying a particular rock proves tricky, ask for help from a geologist with a state university or natural history museum.

KEEP SAFE

Always have an adult with you when you go exploring. Ask for the adult's help when you use tools, and wear goggles when you use a hammer or chisel.

ROCK-HARD FACT

Many places around the world, including most US states, have dig sites. You can bring your family and your rock collecting gear, and take home rock samples for a small fee.

MAKE THEM SHINE!

Bring out the beauty of your rocks by dabbing petroleum jelly on a cotton cloth or old towel and rubbing it evenly over the entire surface of the rock.

DO-IT-YOURSELF ROCK WEATHERING

Have you ever seen an old barn that's barely standing? It shows the effects of years of exposure to the rain, wind, and sun. Even though rocks are much harder than the wood in old barns, they also experience the effects of **weathering**.

BIOLOGICAL WEATHERING

You've probably seen a plant or tree root that breaks through a sidewalk. This is an example of **biological** weathering. Tree roots can crack rocks, and slow-growing organisms such as lichen can break down rocks and even change their composition.

CHEMICAL WEATHERING

Rocks also undergo change through chemical weathering. Water, acids, and gases slowly dissolve or react with minerals in the rock, creating new compounds. Would you like to recreate this process? Take a look at the experiment on the next page.

ACID TEST

Let's apply lemon juice and vinegar—weak acids found in most kitchens—to two of your rocks. What do you think will happen?

GET YOUR PARENT'S PERMISSION BEFORE STARTING THIS PROJECT!

WHAT TO DO

1 Put a few drops of lemon juice on one rock.

2 Put a few drops of vinegar on the second rock.

3 Listen carefully!

WHAT HAPPENS NEXT?

Did you hear a fizzing sound? Lemon juice and vinegar contain acetic acid, which dissolves calcium carbonate. Acetic acid will cause limestone, chalk, or calcite to fizz.

STRANGE-BUT-TRUE STORIES
MENACING METEORITES!

VREDEFORT CRATER FROM SPACE

INSIDE VREDEFORT CRATER

Most meteors burn up as they enter Earth's atmosphere. Despite that, about 500 meteorites hit Earth's surface each year. These impacts can be deadly, killing everything and everyone around them. Many scientists believe a meteorite impact caused the dinosaurs to become extinct.

The biggest impact crater, Vredefort Crater in South Africa, measures about 236 miles (380 km) in diameter. It is so large that it can only be seen in full from space.

Scientists say a house-sized meteorite could flatten buildings for miles around. But even smaller ones can shatter windows as they enter our atmosphere or cause burns from the light energy they release.

MOON ROCKS! MARS ROCKS!

Astronauts from NASA's Apollo Moon missions brought back more than 800 pounds (363 kg) of **lunar** rock for scientists to study. Interestingly, the samples were common to our planet—rocks like basalt, anorthosite, and breccia. But unlike their earthly counterparts, lunar rocks are worth millions of dollars each.

Scientists are also studying the rocks on Mars using NASA's unmanned rovers. Some of Mars's surface looks much like the sandstone found in the Southwestern United States. Other areas are covered in sedimentary mudstone, hinting at an ancient bed of water.

MOON ROCK

ROCK-HARD FACT

Impact craters on Earth's surface get weathered or eroded over time. But craters on the Moon look just like they did the day they happened. That's because the Moon doesn't have weather, water, and plants as Earth does.

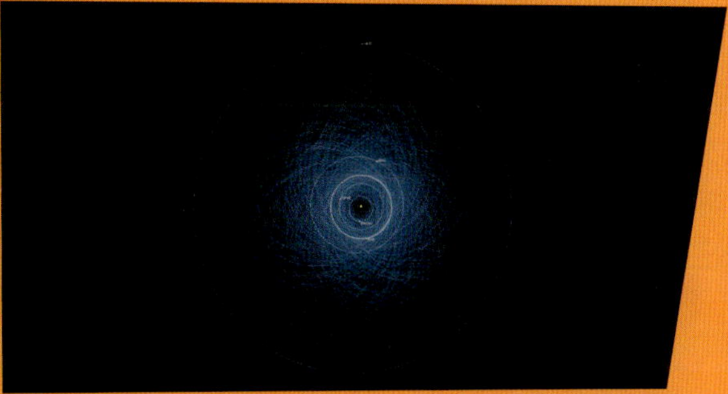

Chances are you've never seen a map like this one. This is a map of what the space agency NASA calls "potentially hazardous asteroids"—more than 1,400 of them. "These are the asteroids considered hazardous because they are fairly large (at least 460 feet or 140 meters in size), and because they follow orbits that pass close to the Earth's orbit (within 4.7 million miles or 7.5 million kilometers)," NASA officials wrote. But don't be too worried. None of the asteroids are expected to hit in the next 100 years.

GLORIOUS GEMS

Gems are like the royalty of the mineral world: They're valued for their rarity. The rarer a gem, the more valuable it is. When they're rough—meaning uncut and unpolished—they may look like pretty rocks, but an expert can bring out their color and fire. Fire describes the way gems seem to flash different colors of light, as if each stone contains a rainbow within itself.

WHAT IS YOUR BIRTHSTONE?

Birthstones are gemstones that are assigned to birth months. Can you find your birthstone?

JANUARY GARNET · **FEBRUARY** AMETHYST · **MARCH** AQUAMARINE

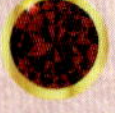
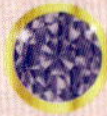
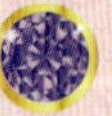

APRIL DIAMOND · **MAY** EMERALD · **JUNE** PEARL

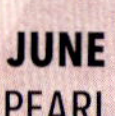

JULY RUBY · **AUGUST** PERIDOT · **SEPTEMBER** SAPPHIRE

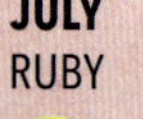
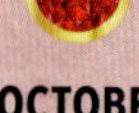

OCTOBER OPAL · **NOVEMBER** TOPAZ · **DECEMBER** TANZANITE

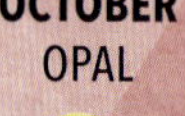

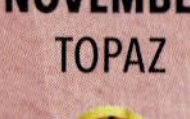

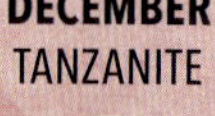

AMETHYST

TURQUOISE

CITRINE

GARNET

SAPPHIRE

ROUGH RUBY

DIAMOND

ROSE QUARTZ

OPAL

TOPAZ

AQUAMARINE

RAW EMERALD

ROCK-HARD FACT

Gemstones are measured in units called carats. One carat measures just a fraction of an ounce, or 0.2 grams.

Scientists have found a way to make gems more affordable by creating them in a laboratory. Lab-created gems have the exact same composition as the ones found in nature. But unlike natural stones, they contain fewer flaws. And because no mining is required, they're also easier on the environment and safer to produce.

THE STARS THAT SHINE BRIGHTEST

More than 5,000 minerals are found on Earth. Of those, fewer than 100 are worthy to be called gems. And of those, an even smaller number can claim star status. Let's meet a few of them.

THE HOPE DIAMOND

At 45.42 carats, this beautiful blue diamond, which is said to be cursed, has a value that's hard to place. Beheadings, murders, and accidents have befallen its many owners. But were the stories made up just to increase the rare diamond's value?

THE BLACK PRINCE'S RUBY

The story of this stone—which is not actually a ruby but an uncut spinel—begins in the 14th century, when Pedro the Cruel murdered its owner, the Moorish Prince of Granada. Pedro took the chicken-egg-sized stone but made a deal to give it to Edward (the Black Prince), son of King Edward III of England. It is on display with the British crown jewels.

THE ANDAMOOKA OPAL

The South Australian government gave this 203-carat opal, considered the finest opal ever found because of its rich colors, to Queen Elizabeth II of England in 1954. But the queen didn't seem to be much of an opal fan, and the necklace was kept in a vault after she wore it only once for a short time.

THE STAR OF INDIA

The size of a golf ball, this 563-carat gem is the world's largest star sapphire. The mineral rutile gives the world-famous gem its milky color and produces a star pattern when light is reflected on the stone. It was stolen from the American Museum of Natural History in New York City in 1964, but was soon recovered and has been back on display ever since.

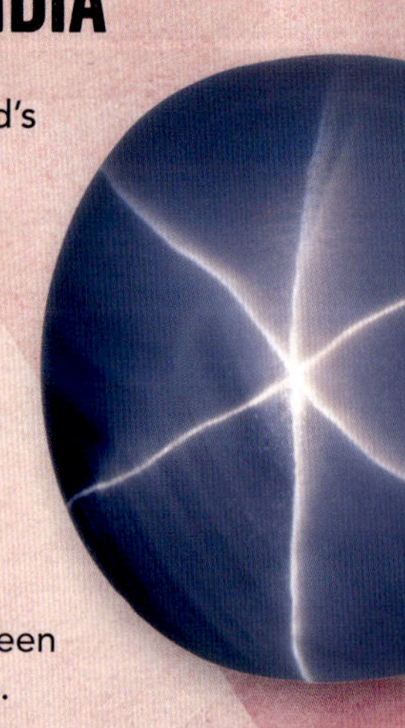

GEMSTONES THAT COMMAND RESPECT

These gems rank among the most expensive in the world.

1 Blue diamond
Up to $3.93 million per carat

2 Red diamond
$1 million per carat

3 Musgravite
$35,000 per carat

4 Alexandrite
$12,000 per carat

CRYSTAL SYSTEMS

If you like minerals and gems, prepare to like geometry! The crystals in minerals and gems are made of six geometric shapes.

TETRAGONAL
EXAMPLE: ZIRCON

CUBIC
EXAMPLE: HALITE

HEXAGONAL
EXAMPLE: QUARTZ

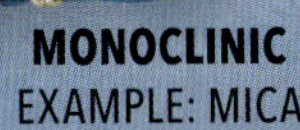

MONOCLINIC
EXAMPLE: MICA

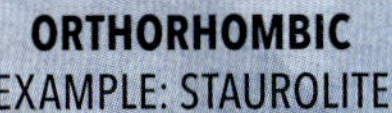

ORTHORHOMBIC
EXAMPLE: STAUROLITE

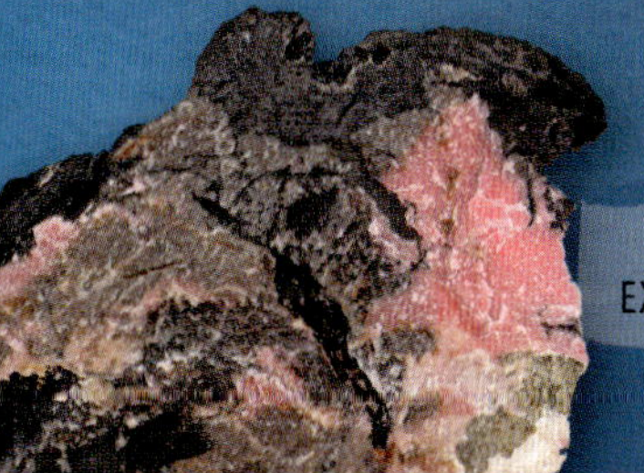

TRICLINIC
EXAMPLE: RHODONITE

STRANGE-BUT-TRUE STORIES
SUPER SAPPHIRES!

Today people value sapphires for their beautiful color, which is usually a deep blue. But in ancient times, they were valued for their supposed health benefits.

People would grind sapphires into powder. Then they ate it. They believed ground sapphires would cure aches and pains, stomach issues in babies, and mental illness. They also believed it would improve eyesight.

Sapphires were assigned other powers as well. They were believed to kill snakes and prevent people from being jealous about other people's property or luck. Today their power is in their prices, with sapphires selling for as much as $11,000 per carat.

ROCK-HARD FACT

Pearls, coral, and amber are organic gems. Pearls are the only gems created by living animals. Coral is the joined-up skeletons of tiny sea creatures. Amber, made from tree resin, comes from a living thing.

GEMS WITH ALIEN ORIGINS

We've talked about how terrible destruction can result when meteorites hit Earth. But so can beautiful things, such as the gem-quality glasses known as moldavite and Libyan Desert glass, or the gem pallasite.

Moldavite resulted from what scientists think was a meteorite impact long, long ago in what is now Germany. The meteorite broke into two pieces and hit with enough heat and force to melt the surrounding rock. Libyan Desert glass formed in the same way in Africa long ago. Pallasite is otherworldly—it comes from an actual meteorite and is highly valued as a gem. Is it by chance pallasite is an alien green? You decide.

ROCK-HARD FACT

Impurities are elements found in small amounts in gems. They are what give gems their colors. Chromium makes a ruby appear red, while iron makes a topaz appear honey-colored.

EVERYDAY GEMS

QUARTZ

Gemstones aren't just beautiful. They're useful. And whether you know it or not, you probably use them every day. Quartz, for instance, is commonly used in making glass and mining natural gas. The mineral and gem is also used in clocks, watches, and electronics. Quartz clocks and watches are more accurate than other timepieces, and quartz crystals can be found in cell phones, computers, games, and other electronics.

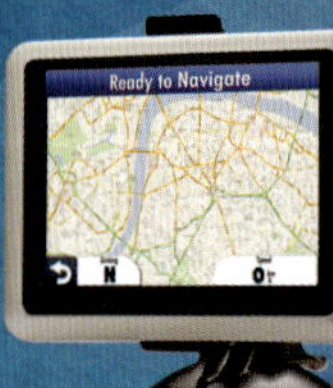

As for diamonds, the most treasured of all gems, only about three of every ten diamonds found are gem quality. Most diamonds are too flawed, oddly shaped, small, or poorly colored to be used as jewels. But their hardness and crystal structure ensure none will go to waste.

Because they can cut through anything, diamonds are used in drill bits and saw blades. The structure of diamonds also helps improve sound quality in speakers. Because diamonds are heat- and abrasion-resistant, they are used to make windows for X-ray machines, lasers, and vacuum chambers. They are also useful in electronics as well as in polishing and grinding.

Ranking a 9 out of 10 on the Mohs scale, sapphires are hard enough to be useful in industry, especially in electronics. Scientists have been making sapphire glass using a compound found in the gem since 1902. Sapphire glass is used in electronics such as smartphones and watches, in barcode scanners at grocery stores, and in the windows of military vehicles. The extra-strong lab-made glass is tough enough to be used as armor to protect troops in battle.

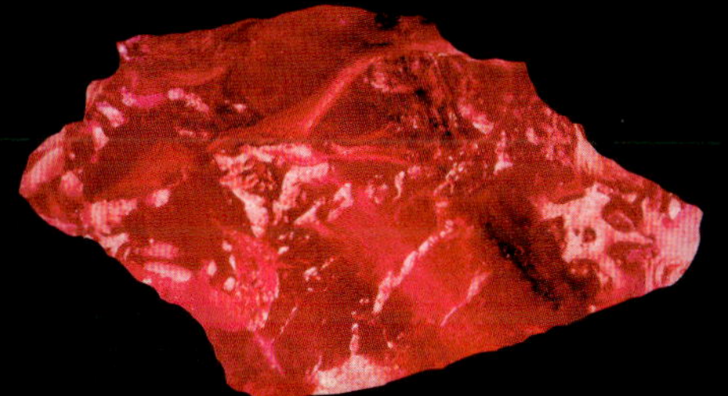

ROCK-HARD FACT

In 1969, a ruby-powered laser beam 100,000 times as bright as the Sun was successfully bounced off the Moon. The laser helped scientists understand more about the Moon, and it will help them understand more about other moons and planets. Modern lasers use different minerals to produce different types of laser beams.

THE HIDDEN BEAUTY OF GEODES

Have you ever opened a plain box and discovered something wonderful inside? Geodes are like the plain boxes of the rock world. On the outside, they don't look like anything special. That's because they hide their beauty inside.

Geodes form in igneous rock, where crystals grow from minerals within the rock in voids created by gas bubbles. They also form in sedimentary rock when mineral-rich water flows into a **cavity** and deposits minerals inside it. The minerals form crystals that build up inside the rock over time.

Calcite crystals and quartz often line the insides of geodes. But that's not all. Purple amethyst crystals can also fill a rock. Some of the more valuable geodes contain opal or gem silica.

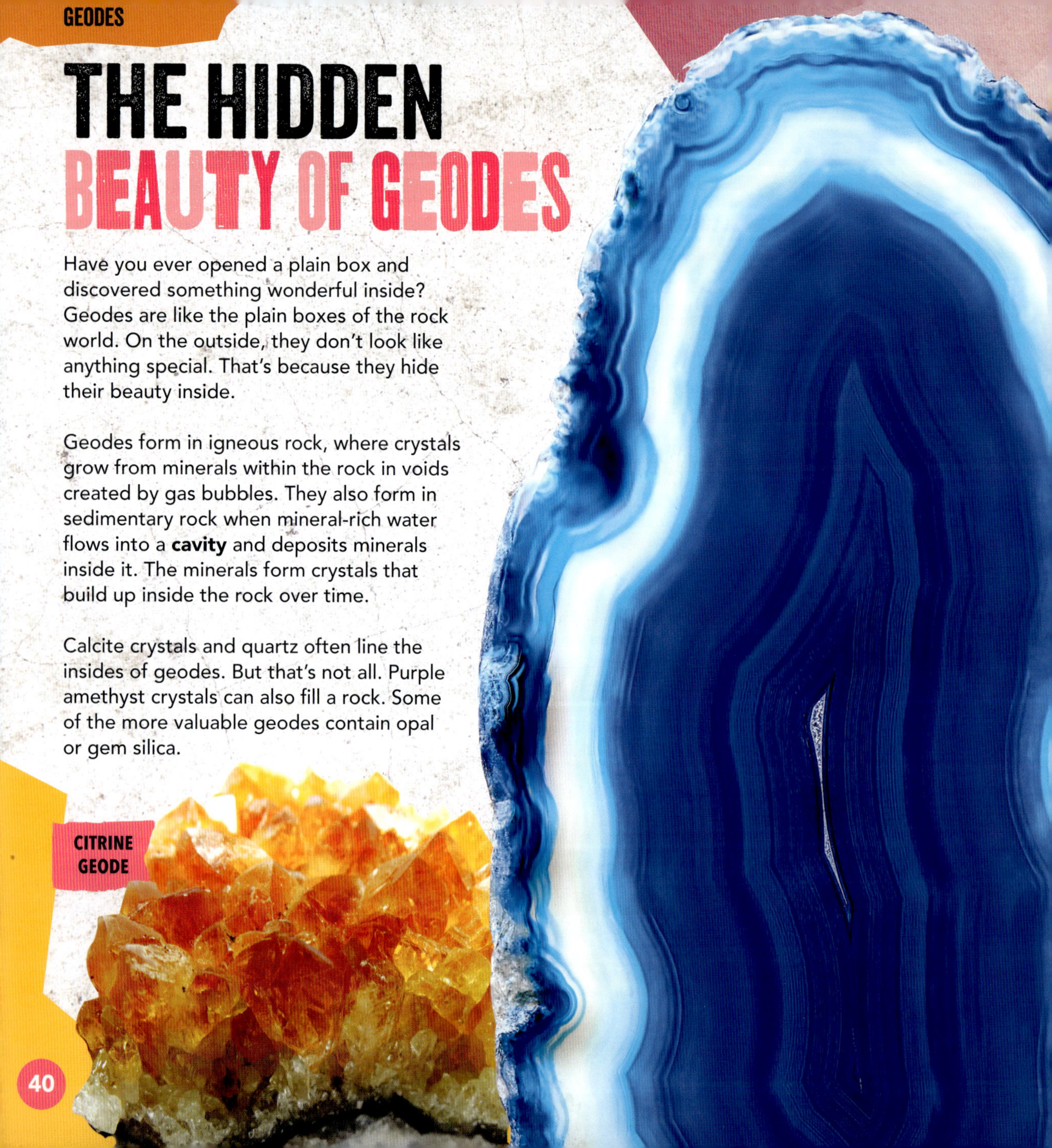

CITRINE GEODE

AMETHYST GEODES

GEM SILICA GEODE

AMETHYST GEODE

ROCK-HARD FACT

Thunder eggs—the state rock of Oregon—are first cousins to geodes. From the outside, they look the same. Inside, they look almost the same. Both are filled with beautiful crystals and gems. However, geodes have a cavity, and thunder eggs do not.

Crystal Cave in Put-in-Bay, Ohio, is a huge geode. While many geodes are small enough to fit in your hand, this one can contain you. Workers discovered the cave in 1897 while digging a well. Many of its blue crystals were harvested to use in fireworks before the cave became a tourist attraction.

STRANGE-BUT-TRUE STORIES

NOW THAT'S A ROCK!

If you saw someone wearing a 1-carat amethyst ring, you might say, "What a rock!" That's how people sometimes describe large gemstones in jewelry. But the Empress of Uruguay, the world's largest amethyst geode, is large enough to make all other big amethysts jealous.

Standing 11 feet (3.4 m) tall and weighing 2.5 tons (2.3 t), the giant geode is filled with sparkling, gem-quality amethysts. It was found in a part of Uruguay where many amethysts are found through mining, but no one had ever found anything quite like this.

The founders of Australia's Crystal Caves Museum bought the geode for $75,000 in 2007, and then they spent another $25,000 to ship it 9,100 miles (14,645 km) to the museum in Queensland, Australia. Once there, it took two large cranes to lift the geode into place.

EMPRESS OF URUGUAY

CRACKING THE CASE OF CRYSTALLIZED CROC EGGS

Geologists don't often find prehistoric crocodile eggs because the shells were too thin for the eggs to fossilize. Instead, the eggs would just break down into the ground.

But in 1930, a fossil hunter came across some unusual geodes in Wyoming. More than 60 years later, scientists studied the quartz- and calcite-filled geodes and determined they are ancient crocodile eggs. Like other geodes, they began with an empty space inside that grew crystals with the help of time, pressure, space, and heat.

"After burial, the interior of each egg **decomposed**, and the resulting void was filled in by calcite and quartz crystals, creating a geode-like structure," a **paleontologist** explained.

ROCK-HARD FACT

There are stories of people finding objects other than crystals inside geodes. Some claim to have found everything from frogs to spark plugs. However, there hasn't been any confirmation about whether these were actually geodes or the naturally occurring buildup of sediment around the objects.

Do you want to take a crack at discovering your own geode? Many states have geode dig sites open to the public. Among them are the Dugway Geode Beds in Utah, Geode State Park in Iowa, Rockhound State Park in New Mexico, and Jacob's Geode Mine in Illinois. Bring your own rock-collecting gear, water, and snacks, along with money for park admission.

SO YOU WANT TO BE A ROCK STAR?

Rocks, minerals, gems, and geodes have many stories to tell if we study them carefully. In fact, some scientists spend their entire lives unearthing the history, beauty, and power found within them. What kind of rock star would you like to be?

GEMOLOGIST

Gemologists are experts in gems. They can identify types of gemstones and determine their quality and value. They often study gems using magnifying glasses or microscopes.

GEOLOGIST

Geologists study materials within Earth and the history they reveal. They also study events such as landslides, volcanic eruptions, floods, and earthquakes.

MINERALOGIST

Mineralogists study the chemical and crystal structures of minerals. Sometimes they work for mining companies so they can collect, prepare, and test samples.

Gemologist

Geologist

Mineralogist

CRYSTALLOGRAPHER

If you have an eye for detail and you love science, crystallography could be in your future. **Crystallographers** study crystals—such as those found in minerals—at the atomic level. They have to be experts in many areas of science and study everything from gemstones to viruses.

ARCHAEOLOGIST

Archaeologists dig human history—literally! They search for **artifacts** and remains that give clues about the people who once lived in a certain area. By studying what they find, they can learn about how the people lived, what they wore, what they ate, and what was important to them.

GLOSSARY

ARCHAEOLOGIST
a person who studies human history by digging sites and studying the artifacts and remains found in them

ARTIFACT
something made by a human, usually long ago

ATOM
the smallest unit of matter

BIOLOGICAL
relating to living things

CAVITY
a hollow space within a mass

CHEMICAL
relating to the way substances interact with one another

CHEMISTRY
the area of science that studies how things are made and how different substances react when combined

CLIMATE
weather conditions in a certain area over a long period of time

COMPOSITION
how or of what something is made

CONGLOMERATE
a coarse sendimentary rock containing fragments of different materials smoothed by the action of water and held together by sand or mud

CRYSTALLOGRAPHER
someone who studies crystals in minerals and is an expert in many areas of science

DECOMPOSE
break down, decay, or rot

ELEMENT
a substance found in nature that is made up of only one type of atom

EROSION
the process in which wind, water, and ice wear away rock over time

EXTRUSIVE
forming on Earth's surface

FLUORESCENCE
absorbing light of one color and reflecting another, giving it the appearance of glowing

FOSSIL
the remains or imprint of an ancient animal or plant preserved in sedimentary rock

GEMOLOGIST
someone who studies precious stones

GEODE
a crystal-filled cavity, or hole, inside a rock

GEOLOGIST
an expert in the study of Earth's makeup and physical history

IGNEOUS
rock formed from cooled magma or lava

INORGANIC
not coming from living things

INTRUSIVE
forming within the earth

IRIDESCENCE
to appear to glow or change colors when viewed from different angles

LUNAR
from the Moon

MAGMA
hot liquid rock found beneath Earth's crust

MAGNETORECEPTION
the ability to find direction using Earth's magnetic field

MARINE
of or in the sea

METAMORPHIC
rock formed by heat and pressure transforming existing rock

MINERAL
a hard material from which rocks and gems are made that is found in nature and is not made of living things

MINERALOGIST
an expert in the composition, structure, and the properties of minerals

MOLTEN
rock that has been made into liquid by extreme heat

OPAQUE
not allowing light to travel through it; not transparent

ORGANIC
coming from living things

PALEONTOLOGIST
a scientist who studies fossilized plants and animals

POROUS
full of holes through which water or air can pass

RADIOACTIVE
releasing or containing radiation

RESIN
a sticky substance produced by trees and some other plants

SEDIMENTARY
rock made of layers of sediment deposited by wind or water

STRATA
rock layers in the ground

THEORY
an idea that tries to explain something

TOXIC
poisonous

UNIFORM
the same throughout

VOLCANO
a mountain or hill from which hot gas, rocks, and lava erupt from within Earth

WEATHERING
the breaking down of rock at or near Earth's surface

PICTURE CREDITS

Cover picture credits: All photos courtesy of **Shutterstock**, unless noted as follows: **aregfly/Alamy:** back of case ml (red jasper); **BamBamImages/Getty:** front of case mc, book cover front mc (diamond), back of case mc (diamonds); **Björn Wylezich/Alamy:** front of case bl, book cover front bl (thunder egg); **Goldminer/Dreamstime:** book cover back mc (magnetite), inside front of case mc (magnetite); **greenphotoKK/iStock:** inside front of case bl (iron filings); **John Cancalosi/Alamy:** back of case bc (pudding stone); **Mara Fribus/Dreamstime:** front of case bc, book cover front bc (blue apatites).

Book picture credits: All photos courtesy of **Shutterstock**, unless noted as follows: **Al Freni/Getty:** 25br (pet rock); **AMNH/C. Chesek:** 34br (Star of India); **A. Telfer/Smithsonian Institution:** 43bl (crocodile egg); **aregfly/Alamy:** 21bl (red marble); **BamBamImages/Getty:** 7t (diamonds); **Björn Wylezich/Alamy:** 41tr (thunder egg); **bubaone/Getty:** 4tr (gold atomic symbol); **Carsten Peter/Speleoresearch & Films/National Geographic:** 13tr (cave); **Crystal Caves, Atherton, Queensland, Australia:** 42r (Empress of Uruguay); **Cultura Creative (RF)/Alamy:** 45tc (crystallographer); **D.NEA Diamonds:** 33cr (machine); **Dorling Kindersley/Getty:** 14–15t (rock cycle diagram); **Ekatarina Fribus/Dreamstime:** 5tr (aquamarine); **Fossil Safari:** 27cr (dig site); **Georgy Shafeev/Science Source:** 39cr (making sapphire glass); **Goldminer/Getty:** 9bl (magnetite); **greenphotoKK/Getty:** 6–7t (iron filings); **I. Huskić, I. V. Pekov, S. V. Krivovichev, T. Friščić Research Group/McGill University:** 12b (zhemchuzhnikovite); **Jeffrey Isaac Greenberg 6/Alamy:** 41mr (crystal cave); **John Cancalosi/Alamy:** 9ml (coltan), 23bl (pudding stone); **Lee Ramey Ogle:** 26tr (rocks in egg box); **Justin Reznick/Getty:** 15br (volcanic activity); **LWM/NASA/LANDSAT/Alamy:** tr & background (Mars); **NASA:** 31mr (asteroid map); **Natural History Museum/Alamy:** 30–31cb (moon rock); **okanmetin/Getty:** 11mc (mica); **Roman Pats/Dreamstime:** 43tr (geode); **Royal Collection Trust/© Her Majesty Queen Elizabeth II 2020:** 34bl (crown); **Royal Collection via AAP:** 34tr (Andamooka opal); **SrdjanPav/Getty:** 44bc (mineralogist); **Universal Images Group North America LLC/Alamy:** 30tl (Vredefort Crater from space); **Utah Outdoor Activities:** 43mr (geode hunting); **Yuri_Arcurs/Getty:** 2m (Earth diagram).